Niobrara

Jewel of the North

by
Rebecca M Rose

{Introduction}

<table>
<tr><td>Visuals</td><td>Sound</td></tr>
</table>

{Music}

The Niobrara River traverses a land of extremes, a place of

stark beauty
stark beauty and surprising diversity, the stage for an epic western drama: the play between land and water, East and West, domestication and wildness, past and future.

"Niobrara"

Niobrara county, Wyoming
Somewhere in Niobrara county, Wyoming the first waters of the Niobrara River reach the surface.

springs and seeps
looking East
Fed by springs and seeps, it rolls eastward through the Sand Hills of Northern Nebraska, flowing over 500 miles to join the Missouri.

clear water
This unique water system supports a crossroads of life unlike anywhere else in the nation, enhanced by high water quality and a relatively free-flowing condition. Many outstanding recreational opportunities highlight the scenic and geological wonders of this place, and the valley is internationally known for its rich fossil deposits.

[www.AmericanRivers.org]
Yet in 2008 the non-profit organization American Rivers identified the Niobrara as one of the top 10 most endangered rivers in America. This river's story brings to light questions that are becoming urgent all over the world: "How do we balance water needs?" "Can individuals, businesses, or states own water?" "Is a river worth more than the quantity of water

dry river bed
in it?" "What is a river without water?" "How do we protect the Niobrara?"

Fade to Black

2

NOTES

PART ONE

"The Flow of Time"

Prehistoric to Present

Visuals	Sound
"The Flow of Time" [title over MAP 1]	{Environmental sound: wind }

Joe's Store
Hat shaping
move outside, hot and windy
"Caution: Rattlesnakes" photo

If you visit downtown Harrison in western NE, sometimes it's hard to tell what year it is. Joe Whiteaker will sell you a traditional hat to keep the sun off, and custom shape it for you. You need a good hat in this terrain, and consider boots. Even today the extremes of this landscape are not to be taken lightly. Wind speeds can reach 70mph, and deliver wind chill at 10 degrees below zero. Summer temperatures can exceed 100 degrees. The availability of water is perpetually in question.

panorama

green valley

Outside of town it's easy to imagine 100 years ago. Or 1000. Head south towards Agate Fossil Beds National Monument; soon you will see the Niobrara floodplain.

Agate displays

20 million years ago, another river flowed through this area. It meandered through a subtropical Miocene savanna, much like the African plains of today. Study of ancient rivers gives us a detailed picture of life in the area, from flora and fauna to weather and natural disasters.

[Learn more about Agate Fossil Beds National Monument at www.nps.gov/agfo/]

This ancient, unnamed river served as a watering hole for a variety of animals, pictured here at Agate Fossil Beds National Monument: large herds of the small camel Stenomylus, three foot tall rhinos called Menoceras, a carnivorous beardog. Palaeocastor, a prehistoric beaver, left petrified burrows that earned the 19th century moniker "devils' corkscrews". In 1885 James H. Cook visited this land while courting, and discovered a fossil bed that would become internationally significant. He married his sweetheart, bought the land, and invited scholars to study the fossils.

Cook photographs

The Cook Family established a tradition of inviting neighboring native tribes to camp here on the banks of the Niobrara, and share stories and artistry. This legacy is continued with the Artist in Residence program at Agate Fossil Beds National Monument.

Dunes close	As the Rocky Mountains lifted, the area became more arid; erosion and deposition occurred, and volcanic activity from the west spread layers of ash. These layers were covered by windblown sand and stabilized by prairie plants, creating the 19 thousand square miles of Sand Hills which lie like a great handprint over almost a quarter of the state of Nebraska.
Dunes afar	
geological examples	The modern river, known today as Niobrara, flows more quickly, cutting through several layers of rock: Under the dunes, the ashy sand deposits became the Ash Hollow Formation, a grayish sandstone forming ledges over the softer yellow/brown sandstone of the Valentine Formation. The porous Sand Hills act as a sponge, recharging the Oglala aquifer and feeding the Niobrara's channel as it cuts through these softer deposits. Next lies the Rosebud Formation, a hard pinkish-brown sandstone. Because the Rosebud formation is a resistant bedrock, water does not filter down through it. Rather it flows along the top until it reaches the surface, springing to ground level in countless tributaries, or seeping from the canyon walls to join the river in its journey east.
Springs and seep fields	
southern banks	
aerial	Behold, the time machine, the spacial anomaly: Cutting as much as 300 feet into the surrounding tableland, the Niobrara River Valley creates a moderate micro-climate, providing habitat for an amazing range of species, protected from the wind and heat of the Sand Hills above. Some 30 miles of the southern banks and canyons remain cool and moist, a refuge for ice-age plants and animals.
Old photographs fossil collections	Humans have found shelter and abundance in the river valley for at least 10,000 years. In the past 150 years people have been cataloging the amazing fossils found in the sandstone walls of the Niobrara and its tributaries, which have preserved 30 million years of time. The diversity of prehistoric remains have made this an area of international importance in paleontology.
Historical Dig photos	
Spring in the SandHills	Life has thrived in this valley for millions of years, all drawn by the same resource: water.

Sandoz Ranch

tall sunflowers

Debate over water use is older than "Old Jules" Sandoz. Renowned author Mari Sandoz grew up with her father on the Mirage Flats dryland south of Gordon. Upon his arrival in 1884, he chose a homestead with tall sunflowers, sure that "where sunflowers grow, corn will grow also." In the 1890s, Mari looked across distant hills at Chief Red Cloud, pondered bluffs where revered chiefs like Conquering Bear were put on their burial scaffolds, in view of the Niobrara River. Old Jules scoffed at his neighbors' irrigation scheme, saying "Take the Amazon River to soak up the sand of a ditch like that."

Marsland

Box Butte Reservoir

At Marsland, in dry years, the trickle is barely reassuring, but the Mirage Flatters eventually got their irrigation system just east of here. Box Butte Reservoir on the Niobrara, completed in 1948, provides water to irrigate 11,670 acres.

surface water diversion

In 1990 the Department of Natural Resources declared a moratorium on pumping Niobrara surface water from the Wyoming border to Mirage Flats. In 2008 the Niobrara between Mirage Flats and Spencer Dam was declared fully appropriated, meaning it could not sustain new applications for water diversions. This ruling was overturned in 2011, and debate continues.

An integrated management plan would help balance water needs in the valley, considering all users.

NOTES

PART TWO

"Continental Crossroads"

Residents and Visitors

Visuals	Sound

"Continental Crossroads"

water over Rosebud

clear water riffles

aerial

Mixed forest from above Smith Falls

prairie life

Aspen stand

Animals

yellow headed blackbird

people having a good time

special needs launch

By the time the Niobrara reaches the city of Valentine, it cuts directly through the bedrock of the Rosebud Formation. This keeps the water clear, unlike streams with sand or silt bottoms, and creates stretches of riffles and rapids appealing to recreational floaters. Considered one of the top paddling rivers in America by Backpacker magazine, it has been called "a mountain river in a prairie state".

In 1991 76 miles of the Niobrara east of Valentine was designated by Congress as a National Scenic River, meriting special protection and recognition. A cool refuge from the extremes of the Sand Hills above, it provides habitat for a great variety of Life. The Valley sustains a unique overlap of at least six distinct ecosystem types: Northern boreal forest, the ice-age relic, Eastern deciduous forest, Western coniferous forest, tallgrass prairie, Dakota mixed-grass prairie, and sand hills prairie. Unique hybrids exist; for example, these aspen found near Smith Falls are a mix between the quaking Aspen and the eastern big-toothed Aspen.

Diversity this intense is rare, and unique hybridization is found among Plants, Birds, and Insects. Fort Niobrara National Wildlife Refuge and the Niobrara Valley Preserve set space aside for wildlife habitat; quiet floaters might see beaver, mink, great-blue herons, a variety of fish, waterfowl and turtles, and bald eagles being sustained by the water. Each of these species and their mix of habitats deserve our protection.

Humans flock here too, to share this amazing river.
Every year a stream of visitors spends millions of dollars on lodging, food, and recreational services and equipment. Much of this revenue flows through Valentine. Studies show that low water levels will reduce visitors and significantly impact the local economy.

Snake Falls

Merritt
[www.nebraskastarparty.org]

[Plan A Visit:
www.nps.gov/niob/planyourvis
it/]

Launch from Cornell Dam

Fort Falls landing and trip up
the catwalk to the falls.
Buffalo Bridge
Berry Bridge
[To see flows today check:
http://waterdata.usgs.gov/ne/nw
is/uv/?site_no=06461500&PA
RAmeter_cd=00065]

Smith Falls State Park

Brewer Bridge public landing
Big Cedar creek and falls
Conner Rapids, Stan's Landing
Fritz's Island, rapids on right
Stairstep Falls

Many natural and historical sites are nearby, including Snake Falls on the tributary Snake river, the largest waterfall in Nebraska by volume. Every year astronomy enthusiasts gather at Merritt Reservoir for the Nebraska Star Party, taking advantage of some of the darkest skies in North America.

Several Niobrara tributaries are very popular for sport fishing, supporting populations of trout and other game fish. Adequate water flow is necessary to protect the recreational assets of the National Scenic River.

The Niobrara is excellent for recreational floating, and accommodates a wide range of skill levels. Visitors are encouraged to be respectful of the wildlife, each other, and private property that abuts the river.

Short hikes are very rewarding as spectacular features are tucked away in tributary canyons. Historic bridges are used for landmarks, and occasional signposts aid floaters in navigation. A gauge station at Berry Bridge records water flow in cubic feet per second, one of a series of stations all along the river to help monitor water levels. This provides data for constructive stewardship.

Floaters often stop to play in the many waterfalls and springs, clean water over shallow rock ledges and sandy banks. It's an unparalleled playplace in Nebraska.

Smith Falls is the tallest waterfall in Nebraska, about 70 feet. This site became a State Park in 1992, with a footbridge, camping and picnic accommodations, and a public access launch site. A Park Permit is only required for those arriving by land.

County Line Bridge

At County Line Bridge floaters leave Cherry county; now Keya Paha county is to the north, Brown county to the south. The floatable corridor is contained in these three counties, though the Niobrara National Scenic River extends a bit further downstream into Rock county. It contains Class I, II, and III rapids, but be sure to pull out before the Norden Chute.

Rocky Ford
Norden Chute

Norden to winter
Ice Jam

Many visitors float a section of the National Scenic River on summer weekends, but there are year 'round opportunities to enjoy the Niobrara.

{musical interlude}

Fade to Black

NOTES

PART THREE

"Conflict and Confluence"

"Conflict and Confluence"

Visuals	Sound
Wilderness	The melding and blurring of distinctions makes this area precious as a unique environment. It's an experiment by nature, where organisms interact and evolve together on the edges of their natural range.
Human artifacts historical photographs	Humans have participated in this process since they arrived, hunting mastodon, planting corn, cutting trees, building dams, loving and fighting with each other.
prickly poppy w/ barbed wire	In a land of extremes, it's easy to resort to "us and them", and human history of the valley is full of skirmishes between tribes, strife between natives and immigrants, ranchers and farmers, tension between business and conservation.
Norden Chute	In the 1940s the Bureau of Reclamation studied this site for another potential dam. The Norden Dam would have stored water to deliver to the Springfield and O'Neill area 75 miles downstream.
old photos, signage, etc.	The project was approved by Congress in 1972. Already, several outfitters were guiding recreational groups, paleontologists were in the middle of an exciting dig, and naturalists were exploring the unique ecosystem, soon scheduled to be under 60 feet of water. The conservation movement sprang to action.
photos scrapbook	Save the Niobrara River Association formed, embarking on a vast campaign to educate the public, and bringing a lawsuit against the Bureau of Reclamation challenging its Environmental Impact Statement. International groups like the Audubon Society and the Nature Conservancy coordinated with local Landowners and Conservationists, Citizens and Policymakers.
Niobrara Valley Preserve	In 1980 the Nature Conservancy, an international non-profit organization, purchased 54,000 acres to create the Niobrara Valley Preserve: approximately 25 miles of riverbank on that cool south side, and 4 miles of the sunny north banks, supporting conservation efforts to preserve this unique crossroads of habitat and wildlife.
Meadville (Ainsworth)	

Fred Thomas Overlook
headlines

Omaha World-Herald reporter Fred Thomas covered the issue thoroughly, bringing the story to a much wider group of Nebraskans as events developed. Several lawsuits addressed safety of the proposed dam, its environmental impact, and economic return.

photos

In 1985 the Bureau of Reclamation abandoned the proposed Norden Dam, saying "it does not have sufficient support". River advocates shared a sigh of relief, but their work was not finished: concerned Nebraskans traveled to Washington DC to testify before Congress in favor of National Scenic River designation, granted in 1991. State legislation and local cooperation resulted in formation of the Niobrara Council to assist in management and protection of the scenic corridor. The Niobrara is the only National Scenic River that is predominantly bordered by private land. Some is leased and managed by State and Federal rangers as parks and preserves. Many landowners participate in conservation easements and other protections of habitat and the scenic nature of the river valley.

Niobrara Council cleanup

Long Pine

Long Pine Creek, near Ainsworth was granted the state's first in-stream flow appropriation, to support Brown and Rainbow Trout for fishing.

[for more about instream flow implementation, see www.nlc.state.ne.us/epubs/G10 0/B046-2008.pdf]

At nearly every turn, the people of Nebraska and the United States have chosen to preserve this unique resource.
Once again we are called to protect the Niobrara for future generations. Now the threat is not a deep reservoir, but low water levels. Nebraska state law allows river water to be appropriated for many uses: domestic, agricultural, power generation, wildlife, and recreation. In years of low rainfall, the demand on river water for irrigation is especially high.

Naper

It remains a challenge to balance the valid water needs of all users to ensure the Niobrara remains a healthy river for all of Nebraska.

Spencer Dam

The Nebraska Public Power District's Spencer Hydropower plant owns water rights dating to the 1890s, requiring water flow to generate electricity for a number of nearby communities.

The dam must be periodically flushed of trapped sand and sediment. This maintenance activity is coordinated with the Department of Environmental Quality to minimize disturbance of animals living downstream, a good example of cooperative stewardship.

Pishelville

Niobrara State Park

the BathHouse

As it approaches the Missouri River valley, the Niobrara becomes broad and braided, the channels weaving and crossing, melting into sandbars and marshes.

The channel here shifts its course often and the town of Niobrara, Nebraska has moved several times. Water from upstream deposits tons of sand per hour, trapped behind Gavin's Point Dam.

As the channel fills in, the water floods the next level of ground, changing it to marshland.

Whooping cranes love this place, and it provides important habitat to other species protected by state and federal law as well. Pallid sturgeon, least tern, and piping plover make their way into the Niobrara from the Missouri, finding precious nesting areas in the sandy and turbid waters and wetlands of this delta.

Paddlefish study

A recent study of paddlefish highlights the importance of the relatively free-flowing Niobrara to Missouri river species. Seasonal water fluctuations are important to fish reproductive cycles. Man-made changes to these flow patterns on the Missouri mean that many fish rely on the Niobrara to spawn. Low water levels in the Niobrara River could devastate fish populations of the Missouri River, another example of the need for cooperation in balancing ourselves upon these lands and waters.

visit the Ponca
[www.poncatribe-ne.org/]
Tribal Museum

Chief Standing Bear memorial bridge

Standing Bear homesite map

The Ponca tribe had lived here for generations when the Lewis and Clark expedition passed through in 1804, and the tribe still lives here today.

Civil rights hero Chief Standing Bear is buried here, near the site of his birth, at his home on the Niobrara.

After forced relocation to Oklahoma, Standing Bear and a small number of Ponca returned to Nebraska. Resisting detention, he eventually convinced a court in 1879 that "an Indian is a person" under the law. Provisions were made for Ponca to live at their ancestral home on the Niobrara, where Standing Bear remained the rest of his days. With this precedent, Native Americans gained recognition of human rights under the United States Constitution. A love of this place brought the whole country closer to its ideal of equality.

channels and sandbars

As we move together into the future, our fates braid and meld like channels and sandbars. Human life is intimately linked with the natural world around it. Our actions are a part of the ongoing western drama, the play between land and water, East and West, domestication and wildness, stewardship and misuse, past and future.

fog/dew

The waters of the Earth endlessly cycle, evaporating and condensing, participating in chemical reactions, combining and separating, facilitating Life. A river's water is more than its current; it seeps through the ground, it floats through the air, it's contained in the plants and animals of its forests and wetlands. To remain Alive, a river must be able to maintain and repair itself. Numerous studies show that natural cyclical processes like ice jams, floods, and course changes are inevitable and even necessary to sustain healthy natural areas.

Our stewardship efforts for the Niobrara watershed must provide enough naturally flowing water to sustain the irreplaceable mix of plants and animals found here.

Protection today will determine the landscape of the future, and whether the Niobrara River will continually flow through it.

Fade to Black

NOTES

{Epilogue}

In 2011 historic levels of rain and snowmelt caused rivers worldwide to flood.
Residents of Niobrara, Nebraska once again left homes, farms, and businesses for high ground, fleeing the mighty Missouri.

The Niobrara flowed through the Sand Hills calmly, much as always. Recreation was affected because tourists stayed away, assuming scenes of destruction like they'd seen elsewhere.

In June 2011, the Nebraska Supreme Court reversed the Nebraska Department of Natural Resources' January 2008 decision that the Niobrara was fully appropriated between Mirage Flats and the Spencer Dam.

The Department of Natural Resources and the Natural Resource Districts are now considering a new method of determining when a watershed is fully- or over-appropriated.

NOTES

NOTES

NOTES

NOTES